6/08

Cool LATIN MUSIC

Create & Appreciate What Makes Music Great!

Mary Lindeen

ABDO Publishing Company

Visit us at www.abdopublishing.com

Published by ABDO Publishing Company, 8000 West 78th Street, Edina, Minnesota 55439. Copyright © 2008 by Abdo Consulting Group, Inc. International copyrights reserved in all countries. No part of this book may be reproduced in any form without written permission from the publisher. The Checkerboard Library™ is a trademark and logo of ABDO Publishing Company.

Printed in the United States.

Design and Production: Mighty Media, Inc.
Photo Credits: Anders Hanson, Photodisc, Shutterstock
Series Editor: Pam Price

Library of Congress Cataloging-in-Publication Data

Lindeen, Mary.
  Cool Latin music : create & appreciate what makes music great! / Mary Lindeen.
      p. cm. -- (Cool music)
  Includes index.
  ISBN 978-1-59928-972-4
  1. Popular music--Latin America--History and criticism--Juvenile literature. 2. Popular music--Latin America--Instruction and study--Juvenile. I. Title.

ML3475.L56 2008
780.98--dc22

                          2007040584

Note to Adult Helpers

Some activities in this book require the help of an adult. An adult should closely monitor any use of a sharp object, such as a utility knife, or perform that task for the child.

Contents

The Music Around You

Did you ever get a song stuck in your head? Maybe you just couldn't help singing it out loud. Sometimes a song reminds you of a day with your friends or a fun vacation. Other times a tune may stay in your mind just because you like it so much. Listening to music can be fun and memorable for everyone.

We hear music everywhere we go. Music is played on television shows and commercials. There are even television stations dedicated to music.

Most radio stations play one type, or **genre**, of music. Some play only country music. Others play just classical music. Still others play a mixture of different kinds of rock music. Just pick a kind of music that you like, and you will find a radio station that plays it!

The different genres of music have many things in common, though. They all use instruments. Some instruments are played in many different types of music. The differences are in the ways instruments are played. For example, the drumbeats are different in various music genres.

Some kinds of music have **lyrics** that are sung by singers. Did you know that the human voice is often referred to as an instrument?

Playing music can be as fun as listening to it! Every person can play a part in a song. You can start with something simple, such as a tambourine. You could then work your way up to a more difficult instrument, such as a drum set. Remember, every great musician was once a beginner. It takes practice and time to learn how to play an instrument.

With music, one of the most important things is to have fun! You can dance to it, play it, or listen to it. Find your own musical style and make it your own!

A Mini Musical Glossary

classical music – a type of music from Europe that began centuries ago as the first written church music. Today it includes operas and music played by orchestras.

country music – a style of music that came from the rural parts of the southern United States. It is based on folk, gospel, and blues music.

hip-hop music – a style of music originally from New York City in which someone raps lyrics while a DJ plays or creates an instrumental track.

Latin music – a genre of music that includes several styles of music from Latin America. It is influenced by African, European, and native musical styles. Songs may be sung in Spanish, Portuguese, or Latin-based Creole.

reggae music – a type of music that came from Jamaica in the 1960s. It is based on African and Caribbean music and American rhythm and blues.

rock music – a genre of music that became popular in the 1950s. It is based on country music and rhythm-and-blues styles.

Historians believe that people in the Andes Mountains began playing homemade flutes, pipes, and drums 12 centuries ago. These are still important instruments in Latin music. But Latin music has also come a long way from its simple roots.

1400s and 1500s. Spanish explorers came to the Caribbean and Latin America. They introduced the native peoples to the Spanish language, songs, and instruments, including the guitar. Native peoples used all of these in their folk music.

1920s and 1930s. Americans began flying to Cuba, the Caribbean, and Mexico. Many of them heard Latin music for the first time. When they got home, they enjoyed the music on their radios and phonographs.

1900

1920

1940

1600s to 1800s. Rich European traders took people from Africa and enslaved them in Latin America. The Africans brought their musical traditions with them. These included song styles, **percussion** instruments, and rhythm patterns. Over time, African musical styles mixed with Caribbean and Latin-American musical styles.

1940s. Latin music was combined with **jazz** to create a new sound called Latin jazz. Big-band music was popular. Latin musicians created their own big bands. They added Latin instruments and music to create the new sound. People also heard more Latin music in the popular movies of the day.

1950s. Brazilian musicians invented a new music style called bossa nova. It was softer and smoother than other Latin music such as samba and choro. In 1959, when Fidel Castro became the leader of Cuba, many Cubans immigrated to the United States. They brought their music with them. The movie *Black Orpheus* also introduced people all over the world to samba music.

1970s. Many Latinos who immigrated to the United States in the 1960s opened clubs in cities along the East Coast. They played Latin music. This appealed to people who did not like disco music. Salsa became popular dance music.

Late 1990s. In 1995, Latina singing star Selena was killed. This tragic event drew widespread attention to Latin music. Latino pop musicians such as Ricky Martin had huge hit songs.

1960

1980

2000

1960s. Chicha music was created in the Andes. The Brazilian song "The Girl from Ipanema" was a hit in the United States. As a result, the tropical music of Brazil caught the attention of more American fans.

1980s. In 1981, Castro forced many people to leave Cuba. Around that time, there was a financial **crisis** in the Dominican Republic. More immigrants from Cuba and the Caribbean came to the United States. They brought their music traditions with them. The audience for Latin music continued t

Today. There are many styles of Latin music. Latin artists keep finding new ways to combine traditional Latin music with other music styles. Spanish-speaking people are now the largest minority in the United States. Latin music will likely gain even more fans.

Latin music includes all of the music of the countries of Latin America. This includes Mexico, the Caribbean, Central America, and South America. All of this music is performed in Spanish, Portuguese, or Latin-based Creole.

There are many styles of Latin music. It includes everything from Cuban rumba to Andean panpipe music. These music styles are similar in some ways, but very different from each other in other ways. Here are just a few kinds of Latin music.

Latin Jazz

Phrasing and rhythm are important elements of Latin **jazz**. It combines African and Latin beats and **percussion** instruments with elements of American jazz music.

Mariachi

Mariachi is a traditional Mexican music. In a mariachi band, musicians play violins, guitars, and trumpets. They usually wear fancy cowboy clothes, including big sombreros. They often stroll around while they play their music, which usually includes many **ballads**.

Latin Pop and Rock

Latin pop and Latin rock became popular in the late 1990s. Latin pop combines the fast, energetic sounds of Latin music with American pop music rhythms. Latin rock combines classic rock music elements with the rhythms and sounds of Latin music.

Merengue

Merengue means "meringue" in Spanish. Meringue is a light, fluffy combination of whipped egg whites mixed with sugar. Merengue is a kind of happy, joyful music. It is one of several variations of salsa music. Merengue is also a dance from the Dominican Republic.

Norteño

Norteño means "northern" in Spanish. Norteño music comes from the rural areas of northern Mexico. Like *Tejano* music, it uses accordions. Like mariachi music, its songs are based on ballads, or *corridos*.

Salsa

Salsa means "sauce" in Spanish. Salsa music is often described as hot and spicy, which may be how it got its name. Salsa music has a strong dance beat. It began in the Caribbean, especially in Cuba and Puerto Rico. In the 1960s and 1970s, it became a well-known alternative to disco music in large cities such as New York and Miami.

Tejano

Tejano is the Spanish word for "Texan." This music began near the border between Texas and Mexico in the early 1900s. It combines the folk music of northern Mexico with the polkas and waltzes of German immigrants living in Texas. As a result, Tejano music often has an oompah rhythm to it. It usually features an accordion.

The Latin Rhythm

Latin music has been influenced by music from Spain and Africa. From Africa, it gets its strong rhythms. Latin music has a lot of syncopation. This means that the typically weak beats get accented rather than the normal strong beats. In a four-count rhythm, the accent usually is on the first and third beats.

1 - 2 - **3** - 4, **1** - 2 - **3** - 4

In a syncopated rhythm, the accent is on the second and fourth beats.

1 - **2** - 3 - **4**, 1 - **2** - 3 - **4**

Latin music usually uses a combination of **percussion** instruments and string instruments. The percussion instruments keep the beat or the rhythm. The string instruments play the melody.

Percussion Instruments

congas

timbales

maracas

batá

claves

güiro

String Instruments

tres

guitar

cuatro

African Influence

Latin music is heavily influenced by African music and instruments. Many Africans were brought to Latin America and the Caribbean as slaves. By the 1840s, half the people living in Cuba were from Africa or had African ancestors.

African slaves could not take anything with them to the Americas. But, they recreated their drums and rhythm instruments once they were there. Many of the percussion instruments used in Latin music are based on African instruments.

Additional Instruments

accordion

cowbell

trumpet

There are many well-known Latin groups, musicians, and songs. Here are just a few of the most popular Latin legends. There are many, many more to listen to and enjoy.

Groups

- Buena Vista Social Club
- Chente Barrera y Taconazo
- Grupo Manía
- Intocable
- Little Joe y la Familia
- Los Lobos
- Maná
- Menudo
- Ozomatli
- Sólido
- Los Tigres del Norte
- Los Van Van

Musicians

- Marc Anthony
- Rubén Blades
- Celia Cruz
- Gloria Estefan
- Selena Quintanilla Perez
- Tito Puente
- Carlos Santana
- Joan Sebastian
- Shakira
- Bebo Valdés
- Julieta Venegas

Songs

- "Bailamos," performed by Enrique Iglesias
- "La Bamba," performed by Ritchie Valens
- "Conga," performed by Gloria Estefan
- "Dreaming of You," performed by Selena
- "The Girl from Ipanema," performed by Astrud Gilberto
- "Livin' la Vida Loca," performed by Ricky Martin

Crossing Over

To cross over means to reach a wider audience. In Latin music, this refers to a Spanish singing star becoming popular in the **mainstream** English market. Gloria Estefan and the Miami Sound Machine were among the first successful Latin crossover musicians in the United States.

There are also reverse crossover stars. These artists record their music in English but create Spanish **versions** of their songs too. This allows them to reach the growing Latino audience in the United States.

Music Production

The way that music is recorded makes a big difference in its final sound. The type of microphone used and where it is placed are very important. The **acoustics** in the recording room are critical.

Recording music is a difficult process. That is why most Latin music artists record in recording studios. A recording studio has professional recording equipment. It also has soundproof rooms. Studio engineers place the microphones and run the equipment.

Once the music is recorded, it needs to be worked with to bring out the best sound. This is mostly done with computer programs that help separate the sounds. This process is called mixing.

This sound engineer is using a mixing board.

Downloading Music

At one time, music could be bought only at record stores. Today you can buy music by downloading it onto your computer from a Web site. You can then put the downloaded music onto an MP3 player.

Sometimes people violate **copyright** law when they download music. Copyright law helps musicians get paid for their music. Some illegal Web sites let people download music without paying. You need to make sure you are downloading music from a legal Web site. Otherwise, you could be breaking copyright law.

It is also important that you get permission from an adult before downloading music. When you download music, you are charged a fee. Make sure an adult knows how much the music costs. And make sure an adult knows the Web site you are downloading from.

Record Collecting

Many people collect vinyl records. Music stores sell new and used records. You can also find used records at garage and estate sales. Many **audiophiles** prefer the sound of records. They believe the sound is warmer and truer than the sound of CDs.

Experience Latin Music

There are many ways to listen to Latin music. You can go to a live performance or listen to the radio. You can check out music at your local library or go to a Latin music museum.

At many libraries, you can check out CDs and DVDs for free. You can watch concerts on DVDs, cable channels, and public television. Here are just a few ways you can experience and learn about Latin music.

Live Performances

Local newspapers usually list concerts. Look in the entertainment section for upcoming concerts. If you are under 18, the **venue** may require that you attend with an adult. Latin musicians and bands play at:

- community centers
- stadiums
- state fairs
- park bandstands
- art and music festivals
- theaters

Music Museums

Visiting a museum is another great way to learn about Latin music. You can see Latin music instruments, hear recordings of old and new songs, and see photos of recording artists who have been famous through the years. Check your local paper for any Latin music exhibits coming to museums near you. Or check out the exhibits at any of the locations listed below.

Los Angeles County Museum of Art

Los Angeles, CA
www.lacma.org/programs/LatinSounds.aspx

This museum sponsors Latin music concerts. Famous Latin music performers play outdoors on Saturday evenings in the summer. Check with the museum for a complete concert schedule.

Smithsonian National Museum of American History

Washington, DC
http://americanhistory.si.edu

This museum's collection includes instruments, photographs, papers, and recordings of all kinds of music, including Latin.

Raices Latin Music Museum Collection Harbor Conservatory for the Performing Arts

New York, NY
www.harborconservatory.org/m_raices.html

This collection focuses on music from Cuba, Puerto Rico, and the Dominican Republic. It examines how it **evolved** after it was brought to New York City.
The collection does not have a permanent home. It is currently housed at Harbor Conservatory.

Make Your Own CUÍCA

A *cuíca* (pronounced KWEE-kah) is a drum from Brazil. It is used in many Latin songs and sometimes in other types of music too. You can make your own cuíca by following these steps.

Step 1

Remove the bottom of the can with the can opener. Cover any sharp edges inside the can with tape. If you want to, you can decorate the outside of the can with paint, stickers, or markers.

Step 2

Put a small square of tape in the center of each side of the plastic lid.

Step 3

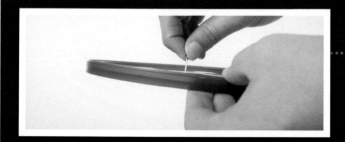

Poke the nail through the center of the lid. The hole should be the same size as or slightly smaller than your stick. Put the lid back on the can.

Step 4

Beginning one inch (2.5 cm) from the end of the stick, wrap a layer of tape around the rest of the stick.

Playing a Cuíca

Wet the square cloth or paper towel so it is damp but not dripping.

Hold the can in one hand. Hold the wet cloth in your other hand and reach into the can. Loosely pinch the stick with the damp cloth. Now slowly slide the cloth up and down the stick. It will vibrate against the plastic lid and make a sound!

Try changing the sound.

- Squeeze the stick tighter or hold it more loosely as you slide the cloth.

- Slide the cloth more quickly or more slowly along the stick.

- Use the fingers on the hand holding the can to press on the lid as you play.

Have fun experimenting with all the different sounds and rhythms you can make with a cuíca!

Step 5

If there is a sharp point on the stick, trim that off to make sure the end is dull. Put the stick through the hole in the lid. Come up through the bottom of the can so that the bare end of the stick pokes out through the lid.

Step 6

Wrap a second strip of tape around and around the bare end of the stick. Make the tape thick enough that the stick cannot fall back through the hole.

Latin Music RHYTHM

Latin music relies on a strong rhythm. Often that rhythm is syncopated, with the accent falling on the usually weaker beats. Different styles of Latin music have different beats. And different regions use different instruments to play the rhythm.

For instance, clave is the basic rhythm of salsa music. It is also the name of a **percussion** instrument that plays the beat in a song. In a clave, the second beat is called the bomba.

Three-Two Clave Beat

1-**2**-3, 1-**2**, 1-**2**-3, 1-**2**, 1-**2**-3, 1-**2**

Two-Three Clave Beat

1-**2**, 1-**2**-3, 1-**2**, 1-**2**-3, 1-**2**, 1-**2**-3

Try clapping, tapping, or playing the rhythms above.

Now try making some changes of your own. Can you add a beat between some other beats? Can you clap or tap three times on a single beat? Play different rhythms on different percussion instruments to see how changing one can change the other.

Want to get even trickier? Try putting an extra beat between the second and third beats.

1-**2-and**-3, 1-**2**, 1-**2-and**-3, 1-**2**, 1-**2-and**-3, 1-**2**

Or try striking two times on a single beat.

1-**2**-3, 1-**2**, 1-**2**-3, 1-**2**, 1-**2**-3, 1-**2**

Write a SALSA SONG

Salsa is a popular kind of Latin dance music that comes from the Caribbean. It is especially important music in Cuba and Puerto Rico. Its strong beat makes it fun to dance to. Its lively, energetic sound is perfect for happy occasions and celebrations.

Like any other kind of song, a salsa song has three main elements.

- **Lyrics** are the words that tell the story of a song.
- **Melody** is the musical notes of a song. The melody is played on an instrument or sung.
- **Rhythm** is the beat of a song.

Salsa Lyrics

A basic salsa song has three important parts.

- The body is the slower, beginning part of the song. It is usually sung by a soloist.
- The *montuno* is the second section of the song. The soloist sings a phrase and a chorus responds.
- The clave rhythm is the third part. See page 21 for more about this unique rhythm.

1 Decide what you want your song to be about. It might be about a party or a celebration at your school. Or you can sing about a neighborhood or family event, such as a holiday celebration. Write down the main idea of your song. Does it make a good title?

2 Make a list of words, phrases, facts, feelings, and other ideas you want to include in your song. Then arrange these to tell your story. This will be the body of your song. You might want to try writing a *décima*, which is a song with 10 lines. Each line in a décima has eight syllables. Many Latin songs are written in this style.

3 Now write the montuno, or alternating chorus. Write a line for the soloist to sing. Then write a line for the chorus to sing in response. Put several different call-and-response segments together to make the montuno, or just repeat the same one several times. The montuno doesn't have to be words. It can be sounds that the lead singer calls out and the chorus repeats, such as "oh-ay-oh-ay."

En Español

No matter what the style or topic, a Latin song is sung in Spanish. You might want to include some common Spanish words or phrases instead. You can use this list to help you.

Bailamos.	Let's dance.
Escúcheme.	Listen to me.
Está bien.	It's okay.
Gracias.	Thank you.
Lo siento.	I'm sorry.
Mire.	Look.
No creo.	I don't think so.
No hay problema.	No problem.
No importa.	It doesn't matter.
No sé.	I don't know.
No se preocupe.	Don't worry.
Por favor.	Please.
Quiro más.	I want more.
Tenga cuidado.	Be careful.
Te quiero.	I love you.
Vámonos.	Let's go.

Son of *Son*

Salsa is based on a folk song tradition. In Puerto Rico, this is called the *plena*. In Cuba, it is the *son*. Son began in the 1500s when words from Spanish poems were set to African dance rhythms. It **evolved** over time to include a wide variety of song styles. Son is sometimes called the grandfather of Latin music.

son montuno – son that includes additional African **percussion** instruments.

danzón – son music played on flutes and violins.

mambo – a combination of big-band **jazz** and son montuno that became popular in the United States in the 1940s.

boogaloo – a combination of soul music and mambo that became popular in the United States in the 1960s.

reggaetón – a fairly new musical style that combines reggae, plena, hip-hop, and Spanish rapping.

Write the Melody

1 Here are some ways to get some ideas for a salsa melody of your own.

- Listen to some recordings of salsa music. These are available online or at your local library.

- Hum some experimental melodies and record the ones you like the best.

- Play combinations of notes on an instrument to find a melody that you like.

2 Practice your melody several times until you know it well. If you play an instrument such as a guitar or a piano, you can play your melody and sing at the same time. Or you can record your melody. Then you can sing along to the recorded melody.

3 Now start matching the **lyrics** to the melody. Sing along as you play or listen to a recording of the melody. You might have to make some adjustments to get the words and the notes to work together. Record several options. Then listen to all the **versions** and pick the one you like best.

Put It All Together

1 First, get your rhythm going. Tap your foot on the floor to the beat of the song. Or use claves or your homemade cuíca to make the rhythm. You might want to record the rhythm or ask a friend to play it. That way you'll be free to sing the melody.

2 Next, play your melody. Keep the rhythm going and match the melody to it.

3 Now, start at the beginning and sing the body of your song. Have some friends sing the response when you get to the montuno.

4 After you've practiced a few times, make a recording of your finished song. How does it sound?

Dance the SAMBA

The samba is the official dance of Brazil. It started as a folk dance. But now people all over the world dance to the 1-2 beat of the samba. They samba in parades, street festivals, and dance competitions. This fun and lively dance can be performed with many kinds of popular music, including Latin rhythms.

Step 1

Get ready. Stand with your feet about as wide apart as your shoulders are. If you are dancing with a friend, stand side by side.

Step 2

On beat 1, step back with your right foot and bend your knees quickly to make a little bounce.

Step 3

On beat 2, step your right foot forward to bring your feet together again. Quickly bend your knees again to make another little bounce.

Step 4

Repeat steps 2 and 3 with your left foot.

Step 5

On beat 1, step to the right with your right foot and then do a quick bounce.

Step 6

On beat 2, bring your feet together again. Bend your knees for a quick bounce.

Step 7

Repeat steps 5 and 6 with your left foot.

Step 8

On beat 1, step forward on your left foot. Use your right food to push your body around to the left slightly more than a quarter turn.

Step 9

On the next two beats, step right with your right foot, bounce, bring your feet back together, and bounce.

Step 10

Repeat these steps for every set of 10 beats. While you're still learning this dance, it helps to say the rhythm out loud while you do the steps, 1 and 2 and 1 and 2 and so on. Take your steps when you say the numbers and bounce when you say *and*.

Make a Latin DANCE VIDEO

Once you've figured out how to dance the samba, why not make a dance video to show others how to do it? Share it with your friends. They can learn the dance too. Then you can have a dance party! Everybody samba!

Step 1

Write a short introduction about the history of the samba. Make or gather any props you want to use, such as a map of Brazil or photos of Carnival in Rio de Janeiro. Read or talk from your notes while a friend videotapes you. This is the first part of your video.

Step 2

Now record the dance instructions. Perform the steps to the dance as you explain each one. Use the instructions on pages 26-27 to help you. This middle section of your video is the how-to part.

Step 3

Finally, record the end of your video. It could be you dancing the samba to show how it looks when an expert does it. Show everyone how much fun this dance is! Or you could say a few final words directly to viewers to encourage them to try the samba. Be sure to remind them that it takes some practice to get good at it!

The First in a Series?

There are many kinds of Latin music and dances besides the samba. Here are just a few.

bossa nova – an easy-listening combination of samba and **jazz** from Brazil.

cha-cha – a mambo danced at a medium speed.

conga – a Cuban line dance that became popular in the United States in the 1930s.

lambada – a Brazilian combination of merengue, salsa, and reggae.

merengue – dance music from the Dominican Republic played on accordion, brass, and **percussion** instruments.

meríngue – slower merengue music from Haiti that uses guitars instead of accordions.

rumba – Cuban dance music featuring syncopated rhythm played on drums and clave.

tango – a close dance of love from Argentina that first became popular in the United States in the 1920s.

Conclusion

Latin music includes moods, sounds, and rhythms from around the world. It is based on centuries of tradition. At the same time, it is constantly being recreated and reinvented by new musicians. It can be joyful and lively or sad and haunting.

There are many different styles of Latin music. Sampling all of them will help you find the songs and artists you like the best. You might also learn about the fascinating countries and cultures this music comes from.

You may even find that you want to make some Latin music yourself! Latin music was created by people just like you. It was,

and still is, created by people who wanted to tell their stories and share their talents.

Latin musicians want to fill their world with beautiful sounds and compelling rhythms. They want to celebrate by singing and dancing. You can do the same by singing, writing, or playing your own music. Or fill your world with music by listening to it and learning about it.

No matter where you are from, chances are there is at least one style of Latin music that will connect with your heart and soul. It might even make you want to get up and dance! Cha-cha-cha!

Glossary

acoustics – the properties of a room that affect how sound is heard in it.

audiophile – a person who is very enthusiastic about listening to recorded music.

ballad – a slow song that tells a romantic or sentimental story.

copyright – the legal right to copy, sell, publish, or distribute the work of a writer, musician, or artist.

crisis – an unstable or difficult time or situation.

evolve – to change or develop slowly.

genre – a category of art, music, or literature.

jazz – a style of music characterized by complex rhythms and melodies and improvised solos.

lyrics – the words of a song.

mainstream – representing the tastes, thoughts, or values of a large segment of a society or group.

percussion – an instrument played by hitting, shaking, or striking it.

venue – a place where specific kinds of events take place.

version – a different form or type from the original.

Web Sites

To learn more about cool music, visit ABDO Publishing Company on the World Wide Web at **www.abdopublishing.com**. Web sites about cool music are featured on our Book Links pages. These links are routinely monitored and updated to provide the most current

Index